Mr Clutterbuck Jones
to the Rescue

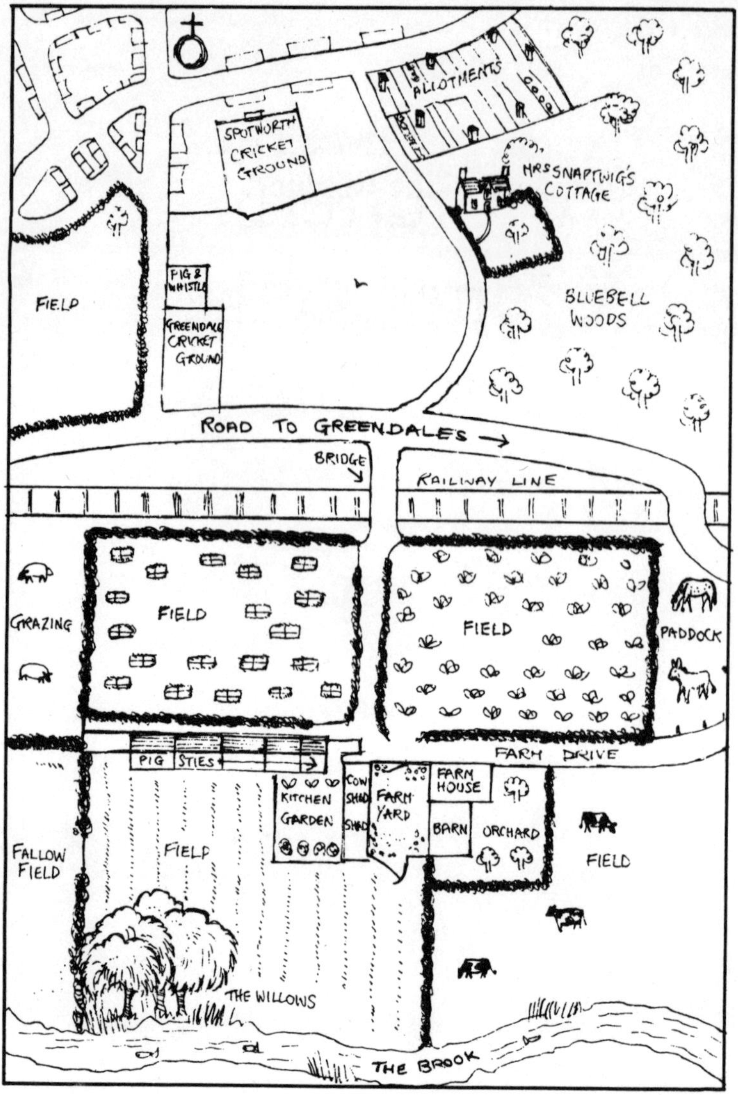

SPOTWORTH CRICKET GROUND
ALLOTMENTS
MRS SNAPTWIG'S COTTAGE
FIELD
PIG & WHISTLE
GREENDALE CRICKET GROUND
BLUEBELL WOODS
ROAD TO GREENDALES
BRIDGE
RAILWAY LINE
GRAZING
FIELD
FIELD
PADDOCK
FARM DRIVE
PIG STIES
KITCHEN GARDEN
COW SHED
SHED
FARM YARD
FARM HOUSE
BARN
ORCHARD
FALLOW FIELD
FIELD
FIELD
THE WILLOWS
THE BROOK

JEANNE GREAVES

Mr Clutterbuck Jones to the Rescue

Illustrated by Linda Birch

HODDER AND STOUGHTON
LONDON SYDNEY AUCKLAND TORONTO

For Dominic and Shar

British Library Cataloguing in Publication Data

Greaves, Jeanne
  Mr. Clutterbuck Jones to the rescue.—(Brock books).
  I. Title   II. Birch, Linda   III. Series
  823'.914[J]   PZ7

  ISBN 0-340-39945-7

Text copyright © Jeanne Greaves 1987
Illustrations copyright © Hodder and Stoughton Ltd 1987

First published 1987

All rights reserved. No part of this publication may be
reproduced or transmitted in any form or by any means,
electronically or mechanically, including photocopying,
recording, or any information storage and retrieval system,
without either the prior permission in writing from the
publisher or a licence, permitting restricted copying, issued
by the Copyright Licensing Agency, 33–34 Alfred Place,
London WC1E 7DP.

Published by Hodder and Stoughton Children's Books,
a division of Hodder and Stoughton Ltd,
Mill Road, Dunton Green, Sevenoaks, Kent TN13 2YJ

Photoset by Rowland Phototypesetting Ltd,
Bury St Edmunds, Suffolk

Printed in Great Britain by T. J. Press (Padstow) Ltd,
Padstow, Cornwall

Contents

	Introduction: All About Mr Clutterbuck Jones	7
1	Mr Clutterbuck Jones decorates his Sty	9
2	Mr Clutterbuck Jones the Gardener	16
3	Mr Clutterbuck Jones becomes a Cider Horse	23
4	Mr Clutterbuck Jones gets a Piggy-bank	32
5	Mr Clutterbuck Jones and the Harvest Festival	41
6	Mr Clutterbuck Jones to the Rescue	53
7	Mr Clutterbuck Jones becomes a Snowball	63
8	Mr Clutterbuck Jones captures a Burglar	74
9	Mr Clutterbuck Jones joins the Carol Party	88

Introduction

All About Mr Clutterbuck Jones

If you have never heard of Mr Clutterbuck Jones, then you have missed a treat and I must tell you that he is very special.

He was born and has lived all his life on Willowbrook Farm in Greendales. He is very big, very fat, very pink and very healthy. Everyone knows that he is the cleverest pig for miles around. They also know that Farmer Simpkins will never send him to the bacon factory, even though he is sometimes very naughty. He is always getting good ideas, you see, and sometimes they go wrong.

You can always tell how he is feeling by his tail. When he is happy it curls tightly like a corkscrew. When he is cross it points stiff and straight to the sky like an accusing finger. When he is sad or ashamed of himself it hangs down sadly like a piece of old rope.

He is loved by all the Simpkins family and except for special occasions the gate to his sty is left open.

Miss Prudence Daintyways lives in the sty next door. Clutterbuck thinks she should be called Pernickety Prudence because she is so fussy about being clean and tidy. She even scolds him for eating untidily from his pig trough. She often makes Clutterbuck feel ashamed of himself.

Chapter One

Mr Clutterbuck Jones decorates his Sty

Now on this particular day that I shall tell you about it was almost dinner-time. Mr Clutterbuck Jones and Miss Prudence Daintyways had been for a stroll round the farm.

'Come in for a minute if you like,' Clutterbuck said kindly when they reached his sty.

It said 'Mr Clutterbuck Jones' in large red letters on the gate which was open.

Prudence followed him inside and lifted up her right front trotter in horror when she saw the mess.

'Good gracious me! What a dirty pig you are,' she squealed.

Clutterbuck's tail pointed straight to the sky like an accusing finger. Oh, he was so cross! You see, ever since Prudence had become his next door neighbour he had tried not to splash his food around. And he had tried to keep his straw inside his sleeping-house and not all over the sty.

'No I'm not. It's nice and neat in here,' he grunted.

'Neat it may be,' said Prue, 'but nice it is not and clean it is CERTAINLY NOT. Anyone can see that you roll in the mud and then rub it off on your walls. To think that someone went to the trouble of whitewashing them for you.'

Clutterbuck peeked out of the corner of one eye. He wasn't going to let Prudence see him looking. His tail still pointed straight to the sky like an accusing finger.

What a fuss about a bit of old mud, he thought.

'Come and look at my sty. It's like a little palace,' cooed Prudence.

'Invitation to the palace from Princess Prudence,' murmured Clutterbuck under his breath.

'What was that you said?' asked Prue.

'Oh I only said, as I bear you no malice, I'll come, Mistress Prudence,' fibbed Mr. Clutterbuck Jones.

The walls of her sty were as gleaming as the day they were painted and Clutterbuck could certainly see the difference from his own. Then his snout twitched. George the pig-man was coming to the pigsties with pails of steaming mash.

Clutterbuck ran as fast as his trotters would carry him into his own sty. His tail curled tightly like a corkscrew. Eating always made him happy.

He was VERY HUNGRY but he knew that Prudence was keeping an eye on him through the railings so he didn't rummage his snout in the middle of his food as he loved to do. Oh no! He ate neatly from one end of the food trough to the other.

She will see that I can be a neat eater anyway, he thought.

He tried to snooze after his dinner, but he could not. His brain felt as though it was racing round in circles, trying to catch an idea that wouldn't be caught. His tail hung down sadly.

THEN HE HAD AN IDEA.

He looked next door and Prudence was nowhere to be seen. She was fast asleep inside her sleeping-quarters. His tail curled tightly like a corkscrew as he crept out of his sty on the tips of his trotters. He went straight to the paint-and-tool-shed. THE DOOR WAS OPEN. He knew he was being very, very naughty, but he went inside. It was dinner-time for everyone on the farm so he knew no one would see him.

He gripped a paintbrush in his teeth and rolled a paint tin to his sty with his front trotters. Back he went for another one and this time he held a big screwdriver in his teeth.

Inside his sty he put his two front trotters on a tin of paint to stop it from moving. Holding the screwdriver handle in his teeth he pushed the blade under the rim of the lid as he had seen George do. The lid came off with a plop.

Clutterbuck's tail curled tighter than ever.

Golly gumdrops, he thought, it's a tin of sunshine.

For there inside the tin was a pool of shimmering yellow paint as bright as the sun.

I hope it's a nice colour in here, he thought as he prised the lid from the other tin.

You are not going to believe this but it's true, it was a brilliant, clear blue like a summer sky.

Holding the brush handle with his teeth Clutterbuck dipped the bristles into the sunshine yellow paint and scraped it on the rim as he had seen George do. He painted broad yellow UP AND DOWN stripes with a space between them all round his pigsty walls and railings. He ran to the paint-shed for a clean brush and painted broad blue UP AND DOWN stripes between the yellow ones.

It was so exciting to see the colours on his walls that once he had started he couldn't stop. So, next he painted LEFT TO RIGHT blue stripes and LEFT TO RIGHT yellow stripes all round the walls.

He stepped back to take a good look and his tail curled so tightly it ached and ached with happiness.

He had a gingham pigsty – like Sally's school uniform dress.

Where the blue had gone over the yellow it

was a bluey green. Where the yellow had gone over the blue it was a yellowy green and there were bits of white showing here and there as well as the clear yellow and blue bits where nothing had gone over them.

He clapped his front trotters together and thought gleefully: Who's got a palace now? Wait till Princess Prudence sees this. I shall like living here. It's a happy home, and he went to the railings to wake Prudence.

Then he heard Dominic laughing and saw him looking into the sty.

'Dad, Sally, Shar, come and look at Clut's sty,' he shouted.

Farmer Simpkins wanted to be cross but he couldn't help laughing.

'A gingham pigsty indeed,' he said. 'All the same, someone left the tool-shed door open again. Your sty certainly needed painting, Clutterbuck, and we can't afford to waste paint, so gingham it will stay until next time. Will you take the things away please, children, and clean the brushes.'

And away he went to tell Mrs Simpkins.

Chapter Two

Mr Clutterbuck Jones the Gardener

Now on this particular day that I shall tell you about Mr Clutterbuck Jones and Miss Prudence Daintyways were taking a walk in the spring sunshine. New green shoots were spiking the farm fields, tiny buds tipped tree branches, and a clump of celandines gleamed with shiny green leaves and gold satin petals. Clutterbuck decided to nibble a few.

'Don't eat them, Clutterbuck,' scolded Prudence. 'They are so pretty and so brave. They have come to tell you spring is on the way.'

'Why are they brave?' asked Clutterbuck.

'Well, everyone wants to pick the first flowers of spring and sometimes they are thrown away to die. And you even want to EAT them,' sighed Prudence.

Mr Clutterbuck Jones felt ashamed and his tail uncurled so he munched a few dandelion leaves instead.

They trotted up the shallow steps of the railway bridge and down the other side. They remembered to look both ways before they crossed the road and they trotted into the cool, pretty Bluebell Wood.

The spring sunshine sparkled on the tiny pale green leaves bursting from their winter overcoats. Delicate catkins hung from branches like golden honey dripping from a thousand spoons. On the grassy carpet the sun spotlighted the bright celandines and wood anemones but the shy violets hid their royal purple in shady, mossy places.

Clutterbuck felt so happy to be alive his tail curled tightly like a corkscrew and a springtime song started to go round in his head, to the tune of Looby-Lou that he had heard Sally sing so often:

I'm glad the sky is blue,
And that the world is new.
From tiny springtime buds
Green leaves are peeping through.

Rummaging and munching here and there Clutterbuck wandered on towards Mrs Snaptwigs' cottage, quite forgetting that Miss Prudence Daintyways was with him.

Now we all know that Prudence is very keen on good manners. So, as Clutterbuck was ignoring her, she politely excused herself and turned back to the farm.

When Clutterbuck reached Mrs Snaptwigs' house in the wood his happiness disappeared like a pricked balloon and his tail uncurled.

Mrs Snaptwigs was in a real state, I can tell you. She was in her garden crying softly to herself and trying to bend her stiff, old back to push potatoes into the ground. And the garden wasn't even properly dug.

Clutterbuck was sorry for his friend and his tail hung down sadly. THEN HE HAD AN IDEA and his tail began to curl again. He nudged Mrs Snaptwigs' legs with his snout. When she saw who it was she said, 'Oh my dear friend, how am I going to plant my potatoes?'

Clutterbuck trotted to the potato patch and back to Mrs Snaptwigs. He nudged her again and nuzzled the garden fork at the side of the patch.

'What are you trying to tell me?' she said. 'I do believe you want me to dig the potato patch.'

Clutterbuck's tail curled tightly and she knew she was right. She took the fork and stuck it only a little way into the hard ground.

'I can't do it, Clutterbuck,' she cried.

But Clutterbuck didn't want her to. After all, he had an IDEA. He banged his side on to the fork and it went deep into the earth, for a pig is very heavy, you know. Then he pushed against the handle and out came the fork with a pile of rich earth. A lovely smile lit Mrs Snaptwigs' rosy face as the tears dried on her cheeks.

'Oh, Mr Clutterbuck Jones, what a clever pig you are. Now we will soon dig my potato patch.'

And so they worked together, Mrs Snaptwigs holding the big garden fork and just pushing the tip in, and dear old Clutterbuck banging and pushing until the patch was all dug.

Then Mrs Snaptwigs raked the garden smooth and neat with her long-handled rake. She tied string to a stick and Clutterbuck pushed it into the ground. She took the string to the other end of the garden and tied it to another stick to show them a straight line for planting.

'Ah, it's all very well, dear Clutterbuck,

but how am I going to bend down to plant my potatoes?'

Clutterbuck pushed the tall-handled dibber to Mrs Snaptwigs then he fetched a potato very gently in his pink mouth and nudged Mrs Snaptwigs.

'Oh, I do believe you are going to plant them for me,' laughed Mrs Snaptwigs. 'Well, I declare I never did know such a clever pig before! It's good to have a friend.'

She walked along the string marker, now

making potato sized holes with the dibber. Mr Clutterbuck Jones popped a potato into each hole, covered it with his snout and stamped it firm with a trotter. And he didn't eat a single one.

Well, what did you expect? I told you he was a very clever pig, didn't I?

They were both so tired when all the potatoes were planted they just fell fast asleep, Mrs Snaptwigs in her rocking-chair on her small veranda and Clutterbuck on the ground beside her.

When they woke up Mrs Snaptwigs made a big pot of tea and gave Clutterbuck the lion's share – or should I say pig's share – in the big old tin she kept specially for him.

She drank hers from her very best cup with the pink roses on it. After all it was a special occasion, wasn't it?

Chapter Three

Mr Clutterbuck Jones becomes a Cider Horse

Now on this particular day that I shall tell you about Mr Clutterbuck Jones worked very hard indeed and he was a big help to Farmer Simpkins.

The farmer had an old-fashioned cider mill and press and with the help of Firefly the pony he loved to make old-fashioned cider from some of the many apples from his orchard. The cider was always put in the cellar until haymaking time came round again next year. I can tell you the farm workers loved it when Mrs Simpkins brought huge jugs of ice-cold cider into the hot fields of hay. For haymaking is very thirsty work.

All the pigs on the farm loved cider-making time too, because all the mashed apple that was left after the crushing was fed to the pigs. It was called the residue and nothing was wasted on Willowbrook Farm.

Residue or leftovers are given to pigs the world over, and English pigs especially like apple cake, the residue from the crushed apples. It is as good as a Christmas dinner to them.

Cider-making wasn't a chore, it was a treat, and all the Simpkins family liked to help. Farmer Simpkins turned the big iron key in the big old-fashioned lock and they all went inside. The cider house was not very big. It was just big enough for the mill, the press and the trough, and the pile of apples, with enough room for the family to get in and for a small horse to walk round the mill.

Farmer Simpkins went to fetch Firefly while Dominic, Sally and Shar filled buckets with apples and tipped them into the mill. Mr Clutterbuck Jones watched happily from the doorway and his tail curled tightly like a corkscrew, for he loved the smell that filled the air as the first apples were crushed and then squeezed down into the trough below. A little song started to dance in his head:

Cider time is the best of all
When juicy apples are starting to fall.
I know how to make it
I've watched it so often,
The stone turns slowly,
The apples to soften.
They fall in the trough,
To be scooped in the press
Which pushes juice out
And leaves me the rest.

He saw Farmer Simpkins coming back, but no Firefly.

Golly gumdrops, he thought, no Firefly, no cider. I wonder what can have happened.

He didn't have to wonder for long.

'Firefly had a thorn in his foot,' the farmer said. 'I've taken it out but he'll be lame for a while. He can't push the millstone round. So that's that, I'm afraid.'

'We can do it, Daddy,' the children said. And they ran to the bar which turned the millstone. They moved it all right, but not round and round the mill. They jiggled it this way and that and grated it from side to side but they couldn't move it forwards. You see they were all different sizes and didn't take the same size steps as each other.

'Oh dear, I suppose we'll have to wait until Firefly is better,' Dominic said to his father.

'But the apples won't be so fresh then, Daddy, will they?' asked Sally the youngest. And she wandered over to sit beside Clutterbuck. 'No cider making today,' she said and leaned against his broad back.

Clutterbuck's tail uncurled sadly and he nuzzled Sally's hand to tell her how very disappointed he was. THEN HE HAD AN IDEA.

His tail curled tightly like a corkscrew. He got up and trotted to the mill. He tried to push the bar but it was too high for him. He stood in front of the bar and looked up at Farmer Simpkins.

'I know you would like to help, old man,' the farmer sighed, 'but you are just not tall enough to push.'

'No, no, Daddy,' called Sally who understood Clutterbuck's ways so well, 'he's trying to tell you that he wants to pull. He knows he is not tall enough to push. Isn't he clever? Let's make a harness for him.'

Clutterbuck looked lovingly at Sally. It was at times like these that he wished his face would make a smiling shape.

What would I do without Sally, he thought, she always knows what I mean even though I can't talk.

They harnessed Clutterbuck to the pole and he started to pull it round and round the mill. The half-crushed apples were pushed into the trough as more came on top of them. They scooped them up with big scoops and spread them on the cider mats in the press. The press also had a pole through it and the children pushed it round to turn the big screw until it was tight against the crushed apples. When the screw pushed the press tight against the mats the pips got pressed as well and added their own flavour to the juice as it dripped through the mats. Then they pushed the pole the other way to unscrew the press, and there on the mats was the apple cake and underneath in the barrel was pure apple juice for cider making.

Mr Clutterbuck Jones stopped for a rest. His tummy rumbled. He looked hungrily across at the delicious apple cake.

Dominic, Sally and Shar scraped the cake from the mats into the pig-buckets and put the mats back for the next load of half-crushed apples. Mrs Simpkins patted Clutterbuck and said, 'It's hard work for a short fat pig, isn't it? How about a bucket of apple cake to keep you going, eh?'

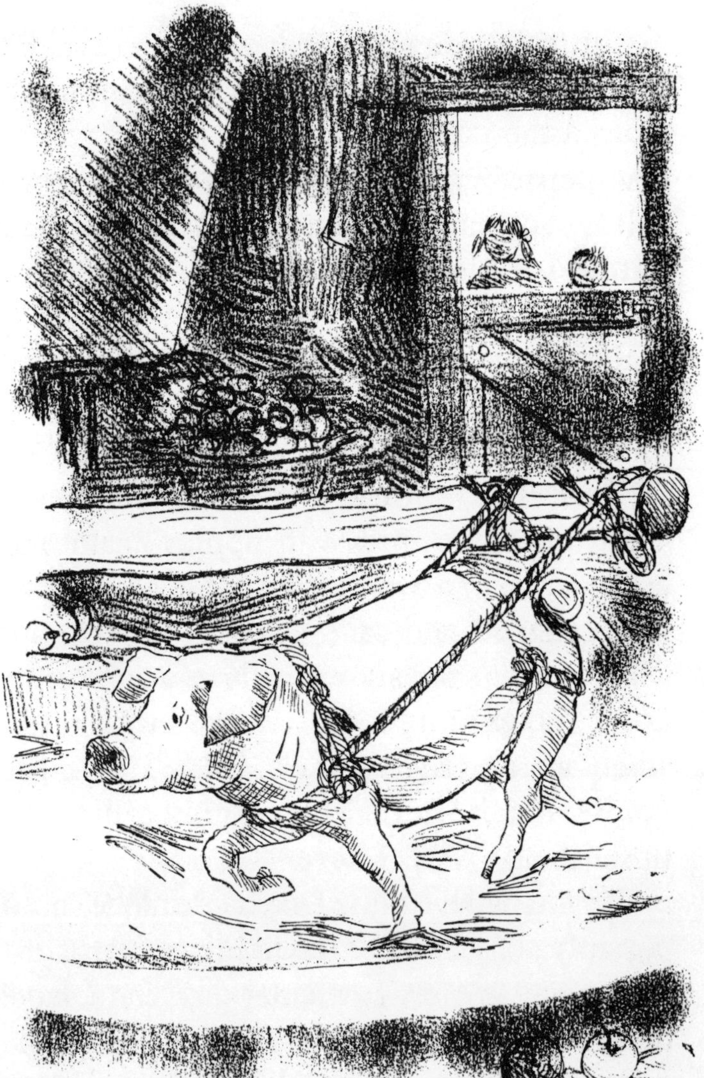

Clutterbuck's tail began to curl again. He was so tired it had uncurled. Mrs Simpkins poured the apple cake on to a thick layer of newspaper because pigs can't eat right down to the bottom of a deep bucket. They all watched Clutterbuck devour the crushed apples.

'Hey, don't eat the paper as well,' laughed Dominic and he screwed it up and put it in the bin. 'You can have some more later.'

'Back to work then,' called the farmer.

He filled the mill with apples again and everyone set to work. For most of the day they laughed and sang as they worked and Clutterbuck's tail stayed curly as a corkscrew as he thought: It's hard work, but it's fun when we are all together. Gosh I love my family. I wish I never did anything naughty to upset them. Well, I never will again.

Do you believe him? Do you think he could possibly stay good *all* the time?

Anyway on this particular day that I have been telling you about everyone was delighted with him, I can tell you.

He pulled that pole round and round and round until his shoulders ached and his little trotters felt like rubber. His snout was too weary to enjoy the smell of the apples, his head felt like a pudding, his tummy was empty again, but did he stop? NO. They all begged him to rest but he plodded on until the last apple was crushed, then he sank to the ground and closed his eyes. He was just dropping off to sleep when Farmer Simpkins touched him lightly on the shoulder with the apple shovel and said, 'Rise, Sir Clutterbuck Jones, Knight of the Apple Barrel.' How they all laughed. But once again you see, Mr – whoops, sorry, *Sir* Clutterbuck Jones, Knight of the Apple Barrel, had saved the day. Is there any wonder that he was usually forgiven after he had done something silly or naughty?

Chapter Four

Mr Clutterbuck Jones gets a Piggy-bank

Now on this particular day that I shall tell you about Mr Clutterbuck Jones was feeling peckish and he fancied something tasty. The delicious apple cake had polished up his taste-buds and made him long for more exciting biting than pig-mash. But he was tired from all his hard work as the cider horse and he couldn't raise enough energy to trot to the woods for fallen acorns, crab apples and juicy hidden mushrooms. He rootled his pink snout around his eating trough and in the corners of his sty in search of any splishy, splashy bits of food from his breakfast. But he had become such a tidy eater with Miss Prudence Daintyways always keeping her eye on him from next door that he couldn't find a morsel. His tail uncurled and we all know that meant he was unhappy.

What can a pig do, he thought, when he's too tired to go food-trekking and he's jolly hungry?

Then he heard the voice he loved most. It was Sally saying 'Hello' to him. He looked up and immediately his tail pointed straight to the sky like an accusing finger. Sally was leaning over the pigsty wall smiling at Clutterbuck and what do you think she was holding in her hand? A fat, glossy pig made of rosy pink china. It had a curly tail and bright eyes and Clutterbuck hated it.

How could she like that silly little pig, he wondered angrily, when she's got me? She must like it better than me, she's holding it very carefully. He turned his head away from Sally.

Sally laughed. Always Sally's joyous laugh was Clutterbuck's favourite sound, but today it didn't lighten his heavy heart.

It's no laughing matter, he grumbled inside himself and he kept his head turned away from Sally.

'Mr Clutterbuck Jones, I do believe you are

jealous,' Sally chuckled. 'Well you needn't be. It's only an old piggy-bank. Come on over here and I'll show you.'

Clutterbuck just turned his head slightly to look at Sally but he didn't move.

'Come on, you old softy,' she coaxed, 'you know I love you best.'

He got up and trotted to her outstretched hand, but he didn't curl his tail.

'Look, it's only made of pot.' She tapped it with her fingernail for him to hear that it was hard, 'and look at this slit in the top.'

Clutterbuck looked, because he was always a very inquisitive pig as you know.

'That is for putting money inside to save for special occasions.' As he still didn't curl his tail Sally said, 'I know you are still cross because you are wondering why it is a piggy-bank and not a catty-bank or a doggy-bank. Well, it's very simple really when you think about it. Pigs like to eat mountains of food and they have big tummies that can hold it all. Well look at this piggy-bank. It's got a big, fat tummy like yours that can hold a lot. But it doesn't eat food; it eats money. Its tummy is saving my money for me. It's Mummy's birthday on Friday and if I didn't have my piggy-bank I wouldn't be able to buy her a prezzy. I've just come here to count it where no one can see me 'cos it's a secret and you are the only one I share secrets with.'

Clutterbuck sighed happily and his tail curled tightly as a corkscrew as he nuzzled Sally's hand.

I should have known better, he thought, Sally would never like another pig better than me.

Sally got all the coins out with a palette

knife. That is the kind of knife your mum uses to mix pastry. It has a big, bendy blade but it doesn't have a sharp edge. When all the money was on the low pigsty wall she counted it.

'Goody, goody, goody,' Sally clapped her hands, 'I've got enough. Now I can get Mummy a lovely present. You see how useful piggy-banks are, Clutterbuck.'

Clutterbuck thought he would like a piggy-bank of his own to keep a stock of acorns in for a special occasion like today when he was hungry and tired at the same time.

He touched the china pig with his nose, walked to his trough and put his snout inside the empty trough. Then he walked back and touched the china pig again, and looked up hopefully at Sally.

'Oh Clutterbuck! You want a piggy-bank too, don't you? But you want to keep piggy-food in it.'

He curled his tail tightly like a corkscrew with happiness and Sally knew that once again she had got it right and knew what Mr

Clutterbuck Jones was trying to say.

'Why don't we make one from my old seaside bucket? I'll paint "Mr Clutterbuck Jones's Piggy-Bank" on it in red letters. You can keep a store of acorns in it for a rainy day.'

Clutterbuck's tail was so tightly curled already that he couldn't curl it any more so he did a little jump and clapped his front trotters together to show Sally how delighted he was with the idea.

After Sally had painted the little bucket she took it to Clutterbuck's sty and he gazed at it in admiration. He couldn't wait to take it to Bluebell Wood to fill it with acorns and crab-apples but somehow he had to settle down and sleep for a whole night before he could go. He kept the pail beside him all night and he kept opening one eye to make sure it was still there. You know how excited you feel when you are going to the seaside next day, well that is how Mr Clutterbuck Jones felt.

The sun was shining when George the pig-man woke him up with his breakfast. Clutterbuck gobbled his mash as quickly as he could, spattering and splashing wet mash everywhere. Miss Prudence Daintyways watched him in horror, but for once Clutterbuck didn't care. He wiped his snout in the straw and picked up his piggy-bank by the handle with his teeth. He trotted merrily along with his tail curled tightly like a corkscrew and a happy piggy-bank song going round in his head:

> *I've got a piggy-bank*
> *Painted merry and bright.*
> *Look inside and you will find*
> *Nothing there, but it'll soon be lined*
> *With acorns and other*
> *Tasty little titbits.*

If you look on the map at the front of the book you will see Bluebell Wood on the other side of the railway line. It was quite a long way for short pig's trotters but Clutterbuck didn't even notice. He trotted across the bridge which goes over the railway line. He remembered to look both ways before he crossed the road and he trotted into the wood with a happy curly tail.

He knew where the tallest oak trees grew and underneath them was a golden crunchy carpet of acorns. He ate as many as he could and then he picked them up one at a time with his teeth and instead of eating them he popped them into his piggy-bank. He laughed to himself when it was nearly full and put a few more from the ground into his already full tummy. Then picking up the pail by the handle he trotted jauntily home.

He knew that cows could bring food back from their stomachs to chew later. He knew that Dominic's hamster could pack his little cheeks with food as often as it was put before him and push it all out with his forepaws and hide it under the hay in his box for later. He knew that squirrels hid a store of nuts for the winter. He knew that children saved money in piggy-banks for later and now he, too, had a store for later.

All pigs are intelligent animals but Mr Clutterbuck Jones is exceptional, don't you think?

Chapter Five

Mr Clutterbuck Jones and the Harvest Festival

Now on this particular day that I shall tell you about Mr Clutterbuck Jones was very naughty indeed. Of course he didn't mean to be but he is a very impulsive pig and he never stops to think what will happen after he has been bad. I expect you are like that sometimes when you go to play in someone's house without telling your mum. You know it is wrong and you know she will be worried but you are having such a good time you put the rules out of your head.

It was Harvest Festival weekend in Greendales and all the surrounding villages. I expect most of you know that Harvest Festival is a big thank you for all the lovely fruits and vegetables our farmers have grown for us to eat and enjoy. In the towns you sing harvest hymns at school and go to a Harvest Festival service on Sunday. It's a bit different in the villages, though, because there are many people who live or work on farms and have large gardens themselves and the harvest means a lot to them. They enjoy themselves for the whole weekend.

The Spotworth Mothers' Union were having a Harvest Pie Supper in the village hall on the Friday night. Other villages were invited. There were freshly made meat pies oozing with gravy, tiny new potatoes, and green peas fresh from the pods.

On Saturday night there was to be a barn dance in Greendales but in the afternoon people were busy decorating the church with fresh clean vegetables, and fruit and flowers, ready for the Harvest Festival service on Sunday. None of it would be wasted. It would all be taken to old people or sick people after the service.

It was quite a hot day on Saturday. Mr Clutterbuck Jones saw lots of people carrying fruit and vegetables and he remembered that it was always cool inside the church. He slipped in through the open door and into a pew at the back. The flagstone floor felt like an ice-lolly and Clutterbuck's tail curled tightly like a corkscrew as he settled down to snooze.

When he woke up daylight was still streaming through the stained-glass windows, but there was no one in the church and the doors were closed. Everyone had gone home to get ready for the barn dance, you see. Clutterbuck knew that no one would come in until the first Sunday service.

I'm here for the night, he moaned to himself, and his tail uncurled.

The floor felt cold and hard by now and he longed to snuggle in the soft straw in his pigsty. He wandered round the church feeling very sorry for himself.

THEN HE SAW THE STRAW.

It was the wheatsheaves that were tied around the pulpit, but he didn't know that. He just thought it was ideal for a cosy bed for the night.

He started to pull it down with his teeth bit

by bit until it was so loose that it all tumbled down in an untidy heap near his trotters. It was just right for his fat pink body to snuggle into. And then it started. His tummy began to rumble like a train going through a tunnel. He had not eaten anything for hours and he was SO hungry. His snout twitched as the delicious scent of fruit and vegetables crept into his nostrils. Rumble, rumble, went the train through the tunnel.

It's no good, he thought, I can't sleep with an empty stomach.

THEN HE HAD AN IDEA.

I can fill my tummy and clear up this mess at the same time, he said to himself. They will be so pleased with me in the morning. I can't think why they left all this old food on the steps and the window-sills. I'll clear it ALL up for them.

And that is just what he did. His tail curled tightly like a corkscrew as he scrunched a pile of new potatoes. He moved along to the apples and then to the cabbages, the runner-beans, the fresh pears and the peas in their pods. Then he ate the bunches of crisp curly parsley, the parsnips, turnips and beetroot. He was almost too full to move, but not quite, and as a pig never knows when he has had enough he started to eat the flowers. He ate them all except the roses because the stems were covered in thorns. His tail curled tighter than ever and he felt really pleased with himself, I can tell you.

There, that's better, he thought, now all they have to do is collect one or two old empty boxes. I'll push them all together to make it even easier for them. Gosh! I bet they give me a medal tomorrow when they see how hard I've worked.

With his tail curled tightly he snuggled into the wheat from the pulpit and soon he was fast asleep WITH THE HARVEST FESTIVAL INSIDE HIM. With such a full tummy he snored loudly and sent the church mice and the bats in the belfry scurrying back to their hidey-holes, and he blew the straw in all directions. Dreams spun round in his sleeping head. His favourite one was when the Mayor put a sword on his broad back and said, 'Rise Sir Clutterbuck Jones. I make you a knight for your good work in this community.'

And his tail stayed curly as a corkscrew as he slept on.

When Mr Snuffledrop the verger came into the church to open the vestry for early morning service his face went purple. He was so agitated that he pecked the air vigorously with his long pointed nose and sniffed rapidly like a train just leaving the station. He clutched his bald head in despair and moaned, 'I know we have one or two church mice, but they couldn't eat all that. We must have hundreds of church mice or a church elephant. Whatever am I going to tell the vicar?'

Just then Clutterbuck gave a huge, rumbling snore. Mr Snuffledrop, still only halfway down the aisle, dashed back to the safety of the vestry. He peeped round the door. He didn't feel very brave, but he picked up a walking-stick and tiptoed down the aisle to the front pews and there he saw the large pink mound moving up and down as it snored in and out on the scattered wheatsheaves.

He ran to Clutterbuck and shouted in his ear, 'Wake up at once, Mr Clutterbuck Jones.'

Clutterbuck jumped with shock, but when he saw the verger he couldn't smile because a pig's snout won't make a smiling shape. But he kept his tail curled tightly like a corkscrew to show how happy he was feeling. Then he had another shock when Mr Snuffledrop said, 'You bad, bad pig. Just look what you have done.'

Clutterbuck's tail lost its happy curl as he got slowly to his feet. Why is he cross he wondered. I've cleaned up for him and now he is angry when he should be pleased.

The verger fetched the vicar who telephoned Farmer Simpkins, then they started to tidy up the mess.

Back at Willowbrook Farm everyone was very busy. Farmer Simpkins ran round the kitchen garden and collected carrots, potatoes, beetroot, onions, lettuce, peas and beans. Inside the farmhouse kitchen Sally and Shar were polishing apples and pears from the pantry and arranging them in box lids and shallow baskets. Mrs Simpkins and Dominic scrubbed and dried the vegetables while Farmer Simpkins took scissors to the flower garden and cut all the flowers he could find. Everyone in the kitchen started tying flowers as soon as he took them in and the farmer dashed off to collect enough long-stemmed wheat to tie on the pulpit.

It was a race against time before the first service of the day and none of the Simpkins family had a moment to eat breakfast or to put on their Sunday clothes.

I don't need to tell you how angry the farmer was with Mr Clutterbuck Jones, do I? But there was no time for anything except redecorating the church. The whole family, the vicar and the verger worked at top speed and do you know, when the people began to arrive it looked perfectly lovely. The scent of fresh fruit and flowers filled the air as Mr 'O-be-Joyful' Johnson played the organ and the congregation happily sang the harvest hymns.

But that was not the end of it for Clutterbuck, I can tell you. Oh no! Farmer Simpkins took him into his sty.

'Mr Clutterbuck Jones,' he said, and Clutterbuck knew he was in for a good telling-off because Farmer Simpkins only called him Mr Clutterbuck Jones when he was cross. Usually he said Clutterbuck, or even just 'old man', they were so fond of each other.

'Mr Clutterbuck Jones, it's off to the bacon factory for you. You are a very naughty pig. I have never been so embarrassed in my life before. How dare you gobble the Harvest Festival food and sleep in the church all night. You have overstepped the mark this time and no mistake.'

Clutterbuck's tail uncurled and hung down sadly and ever so many tears poured from his little piggy eyes.

If only I could talk, he thought, I could tell them that I was doing my good deed for the day and cleaning up. Everybody knows a church is not a greengrocer's shop and I didn't know about Harvest Festival.

Sally was leaning over the pigsty wall. She understood Clutterbuck better than anyone.

'Oh look, Daddy,' she wailed, 'look how sad he is. I bet he didn't even know he was being naughty. I bet he thought he was clearing all the silly old turnips and carrots and things away. He didn't even know about the Harvest Festival because I forgot to tell him. So it's my fault really. So please don't send him to the bacon factory.'

Clutterbuck tried to curl his tail a little bit to show that he was happy that Sally understood and he nuzzled his snout in her hand.

Farmer Simpkins relented. He realised that Sally was probably right.

'All right, Clutterbuck, no bacon factory this time. But you will be locked in your sty for three days and you will only have potato-peelings and none of your favourite food. Perhaps that will teach you to think before you GOBBLE. Come along, Sally.'

And they went into the farmhouse for a very late breakfast.

Chapter Six

Mr Clutterbuck Jones to the Rescue

Now on this particular day that I shall tell you about Mr Clutterbuck Jones was a hero. When I tell you about it I just know that you will be very proud of him.

It was fair time in Grassington. Grassington is the nearest big town to Greendales and everyone looked forward to the October Fair. Children from all the surrounding villages and small towns emptied their piggy-banks and counted the pennies excitedly because they just knew that their mums and dads would take them. Clutterbuck tried to be happy for Sally, Shar and Dominic, but he simply couldn't make his tail curl. You see he wanted to go to the fair. He loved the noisy music, the roundabouts, the happy faces and all the tit-bits that people gave him. But it wasn't long since the Harvest Festival and he didn't think Farmer Simpkins would take him. But he had reckoned without Sally.

She was at that moment trying to persuade her father to let her take him.

'Oh please, Daddy, he won't be naughty when he is with me and anyway I'll have him on a lead so that he can't wander off. You know how everyone loves to see him at the fair, eating candy floss, banging the weight up the pole with his broad back and ringing the bell at the top. He's as good as the fair for making people feel happy.'

'You are absolutely right of course,' smiled her father, 'so put him on a lead and off we go.'

The fair was full of happy faces, bright lights, gay music and chattering people. Right at the very entrance to the fair there were lovely things to eat. There was nourishing, fresh liquorice root tied in bundles. As you chewed the juice out the stringy roots polished and sharpened your teeth. Farmer Simpkins bought a bundle to share and gave a piece to Clutterbuck. The next stall had fresh rosy pomegranates and the farmer bought one each for the three children.

There were huge barrels filled with tiny pieces of cork and packed tight with bunches of purple and green grapes. It was like a lucky dip. You put your hand in and wriggled it around until you found a stem and pulled out a luscious bunch of grapes. Then you bartered with the stallholder for the price. There was the swooning, treacly smell of brandy-snap. The brandy-snap lady worked pell-mell, twisting the soft, sticky circles round a wooden spoon handle before they hardened. By the time you bought a bag the brandy-snap was cold and brittle and snapped, crackled and popped as you took a bite.

Then you let it lay on your tongue for a moment while the flavour flooded your mouth. Then, of course, there was the sugar spun very, very fast into a mass of fine threads. A few drops of colouring, a thin stick held against the whirling side until out came a cloud of coloured cotton-wool. I know you have guessed what it was and you are right. It was candy floss, number one favourite.

There were sideshows all round the edges of the fairground. It is very difficult to knock a coconut off with a wooden ball and only Dominic won a hard, brown coconut with all the promise inside. At the hoopla stall Mrs Simpkins won two goldfish, so she bought a bowl to put them in and some ants' eggs to feed them.

All this time Sally had Clutterbuck on his lead and although he was very good and sat quietly at her feet while she had turns at the stalls his tail was beginning to uncurl a bit. It soon curled tightly like a corkscrew when they took him to the test-your-strength pole. A crowd soon gathered round at the sound of the bell which is so hard to ring. Strong farm workers had been trying with a hammer all day. Clutterbuck simply banged his broad fat side on to the anvil at the bottom and the weight zoomed up the pole to ring the bell. This was good for business and the man let him have twenty free goes and then most of the men wanted to see if they could beat the pig and they were queueing up to pay for a turn.

Next they went to the dodgems which was Clutterbuck's favourite. He loved to watch, but he would have liked it even better if he could have had a ride like everyone else. Actually he thought he would be rather good at it because he fancied himself as a famous rally driver. As always Sally tried to sneak him in for a ride. She had managed it when he was a tiny piglet, but he was big and easy to see now. She was walking to an empty car with Clutterbuck on a lead when the attendant shouted, 'No pigs allowed. Sorry.'

She took him to the side and tied him to the railings. The Simpkins family had three cars between them and had a lovely time dodging and bumping. When the ride had finished all the cars except one stopped and that one just kept on going. At first those who were watching laughed and Sally and Shar, who were in the runaway car, thought it was fun and an extra ride.

The attendant jumped on the side of the little red car and tried to unhook the rod from the overhead track. It just zoomed around, with the attendant, Sally and Shar zooming with it. He jumped off and tried to slow the car by hanging on to it, but he was not strong enough and the little red car zig-zagged round the empty rink. Shar steered so that they didn't bump the empty cars at the side. They weren't afraid, they were having fun, but of course no one else could ride on the dodgems.

Clutterbuck's tail pointed stiff and straight to the sky like an accusing finger. He was angry that all the people were afraid to run on to the rink to stop the runaway car.

I'm not afraid, he thought. If only I could get out there. He gave such an enormous tug to his lead that it came off the fence and he trotted on to the rink.

'Get that pig off here,' shouted the attendant, 'I have enough to do without a pig getting in my way.'

Sally and Shar knew that Clutterbuck would help them, but they didn't know how. Shar steered carefully so that she dodged and didn't bump Clutterbuck who seemed to be running this way and that. Sally was watching him very closely and she suddenly shouted above the noise to Shar, 'Look! He keeps running to the empty parked cars and then to us and then back to the parked cars.'

Shar steered to the fence and went in between the parked cars. Clutterbuck trotted after them and as soon as they got in amongst the cars he lay down behind the runaway car so that it could not move backwards. It was trapped between the fence and Clutterbuck.

The attendant stood beside the little red car and because it did not move he was able to unhook the rod from the overhead track. He patted Clutterbuck and the crowd cheered.

'What's his name, Miss?' he asked Shar.

She told him.

'You are a very brave pig, Mr Clutterbuck Jones,' he said. 'You can have as many free rides as you like as a reward and your family can take turns with you.'

Clutterbuck's tail curled tightly like a corkscrew and a little song about a rally driver started going round in his head:

> *Get on to the race track*
> *Early in the morning,*
> *See the slinky racing-cars*
> *All in a row.*
> *Man upon the platform*
> *Waves his little flagstick,*
> *Brrrm, brrrm, brrrm, brrrm,*
> *Off we go!*

Gosh, I wish I had some goggles and a helmet, he thought. He walked to a yellow car, and the sides are open as you know, so although it was a bit of a squeeze he managed to walk in and sit on the low seat. He put his cloven hooves on the steering-wheel, but Farmer Simpkins knew that they would keep slipping off so he tied one on to the wheel with his scarf and the other with his tie. Mr Clutterbuck Jones, ace rally driver, was ready to go.

Brrrm, brrrm, thought Clutterbuck and they were off. He soon got the hang of it for he had always had a marvellous sense of direction and he dodged in and out, never bumping anyone.

Dominic, Sally and Shar all had a turn with Clutterbuck, but still he didn't want to stop. The dodgem-car owner didn't want him to stop either. It was very good for trade, you see. People were queueing up for a ride in the hope of bumping the pig. And the rest loved watching Mr Clutterbuck Jones dodging around in the little yellow car. Well YOU would, wouldn't you?

The Simpkins family were all very proud of their brave and intelligent pig.

'Aren't you glad you let Clutterbuck come, Daddy?' asked Sally. 'If he hadn't been there we might be whizzing round the dodgem rink for ever.'

She might have been right, you know.

Chapter Seven

Mr Clutterbuck Jones becomes a Snowball

Now on this particular day that I shall tell you about the countryside was covered in a thick white blanket and tree branches were like bandaged fingers. I know you have guessed what it was and you are right. It had been snowing all night.

Mr Clutterbuck Jones woke up in his nice warm sleeping-quarters. He rolled around happily in his bed of straw. He rolled over on to his back and stretched his little legs and he felt glad to be alive, as he did at the beginning of every day.

Gosh, he thought, this is the life! I've had a long sleep with lovely dreams, a good stretch and now it is nearly breakfast-time. Who could ask for anything more? And his tail curled happily.

BUT as soon as he put his snout outside his

bedroom door he knew there would be something more today. He sniffed the cold clean air and gazed with delight at the gleaming whiteness of the snow balanced so gracefully on top of his pigsty walls and balanced even more gracefully on every branch and tiny twig of the leafless trees that he could see. The sky seemed to be spun with delicate black and white lace. I expect that is what you think when you look up at snow-trimmed trees.

He was soon disappointed though. He turned round to look for his breakfast. Instead of steaming hot mash to warm him up like porridge does for you, he found a trough full of snow.

I like snow, he thought, but not for breakfast. His tail uncurled sadly. Then he heard the sound of metal shovels scraping and clanking outside the sty and soon George the pig-man popped his head over the wall and said, 'Breakfast any minute now, Mr Clutterbuck Jones. We had to clear a pathway to the sties first.'

And sure enough, two gleaming pails of

steaming bran were soon put down beside the snow-filled trough. George tipped the snow out of the trough and plopped the pig-food in. Clutterbuck ruffled his snout into its depths to find the hidden treats. Potato and carrot peelings, cabbage stalks, bruised apples and dinner left-overs were all boiled with the bran to make a pig's perfect breakfast with crunchy pig cubes scattered over the top.

Clutterbuck's tail curled tightly like a corkscrew as he munched happily from one end of the trough to the other until there was not a speck of food to be seen and the sides of the trough were as clean as a whistle.

And you know how clean and shiny a whistle is.

He left the pigsty and trotted down the paths that were cleared of snow to the farmhouse and knocked on the door with one cloven hoof. When Sally looked out he did a little jig on his four trotters and she knew at once that he meant, 'Come outside and play with me in the snow'.

'We're all coming out,' she laughed. 'Just

wait there until we get the sledges and our warm clothes.'

Mr Clutterbuck Jones danced a little jig again because he knew that the best fun-time of the whole year was about to start on Holly Knoll, the steep hill that was used for sledge runs.

People were already on the Knoll when the Simpkins family arrived and when Clutterbuck saw the happy, energetic crowd his tail curled tightly like a corkscrew and so many songs raced around in his head he couldn't separate one of them. He looked at the laughing, rosy faces beneath the gaily-coloured bobble-caps. He looked at the warm, bright scarves flying behind the sledges, the brilliant anoraks and the wellingtons of all colours and sizes and he wished he could sing out loud, so happy did he feel. So he zizzed and grunted rhythmically and jumped up and clicked his trotters once or twice to get in the mood.

It was a hard pull to the top of Holly Knoll, which had got its name because of the holly trees on both sides of the hill and in the valley at the bottom. The trees were absolutely laden with pillar-box red berries. There is nothing like colour for cheering people up. Holly Knoll was as bright as a bonfire and the day seemed much warmer.

Mr Clutterbuck Jones had his own way of speeding down the hill. He used his cloven hooves like skates and, because there were four of them and because he was very heavy, balancing was easy. Up and down he went, up and down, but it was very tiring to trudge uphill after every slide down. After a while he lay down in the snow at the top. He was very good at catnapping, sorry, pignapping, and he was soon fast asleep. Now you all know that he dreams lovely adventures when he is asleep and so he did this time. He snored and whistled and slept and dreamed and snored and whistled and slept and dreamed.

When Mrs Simpkins looked round and could not see him she began to worry because she knew that he was an expert at finding trouble.

'Clutterbuck has wandered off,' she shouted to her children, 'we'll have to find him before trouble does. Come on.'

He was easy to find at the top of the hill just beyond the sledge run.

'Just leave him there. We know where he is when he's sleeping and he'll sleep for hours,' Mrs Simpkins said.

'He'll freeze,' moaned kind Sally.

Dominic giggled. 'No, he won't,' he said. 'A pig's skin is warm as fresh toast and waterproof AND he's got his blanket on. Come on, let's sledge.'

Mr Clutterbuck Jones had an exciting dream about rolling down the hill. When he woke up he thought: What a good idea that dream was, I think I'll have a go. He went carefully just over the edge where the snow was deep and lay down on his side, gave a push with his trotters and he was off. He roly-polyed all the way down to the bottom. I know you have guessed what happened and you are right. The snow roly-polyed with him, wrapping him up like a big swiss-roll. But he couldn't stop and he had a long way to go. More and more snow rolled with him. Children on the hill, pulling their sledges to the top or whizzing down, laughed at the huge snowball and got out of its way. They wondered who had started rolling it down, but they didn't know there was someone inside it!

When Mr Clutterbuck Jones bumped to a stop at the bottom he was just one giant snowball. After all he was very big and fat before the snow wrapped round him. All you could see of him was a little bit of snout snuffling from one side of the snowball and a tail with no curl in it from the other. He couldn't move but luckily he could breathe.

He groaned. This is pig-in-the-middle all

right, he thought. It looks as though I shall have to stay pig-in-the-middle too, because no one is going to find me here. I bet I freeze to death while everyone is looking for me. I can't squeal to let them know this snowball is me. I can't even see if there is anyone about. He thought and he thought and he thought until his head hurt. But for the first time in his life HE DID NOT HAVE AN IDEA.

Sally was enjoying herself but after a time she remembered Clutterbuck and went to see if he was still sleeping. She called to her brother and sister, 'Dominic, Shar, Clutterbuck has disappeared. We'd better find him before he gets into trouble.'

They looked amongst the holly bushes

growing beside the hill, but it was not until they reached the bottom that Sally gave a little squeal. 'Look, there's something moving on the big snowball.'

I know you have guessed what she could see. It was Clutterbuck's tail trying to move a bit to keep it warm.

'It's not a snowball at all. It's Mr Clutterbuck Jones,' she called to Dominic and Shar. She walked all the way round the giant snowball until she saw the tip of a pink snout poking out. Dominic and Shar ran laughing towards their little sister, thinking how silly she was to imagine a snowball could be Mr Clutterbuck Jones. It didn't look a bit like a pig. They soon stopped laughing when they saw the tail at one side and the snout tip at the other.

Clutterbuck was so very heavy that the snow had pressed hard against him and harder and harder as he rolled further down the hill. Now the giant snowball was as hard as mud after you have baked mud-pies in the hot sun. It took a lot of people a long time to scrape and scratch the hard-packed snowball open. But at last he was free. He tried to curl his tail to show how happy he was, but do you know, he couldn't. It was frozen stiff and straight like an accusing finger and that was a very disappointing thing for happy Mr Clutterbuck Jones. So he tried to nuzzle Sally's hand to say thank you, but he couldn't do that either because his pink snout was blue and frozen too.

'We'd better get him home straight away and warm him up,' Mrs Simpkins decided. So she and Sally left Dominic and Shar to their sledging and took Clutterbuck home.

They brushed him well with his pig-brush to get his blood circulating. They gave him a dose of cod-liver oil so that he wouldn't catch cold, then they took him into his sleeping-quarters. As he lay down on the straw they piled more on top of him to make him really cosy. Then they left him to sleep.

Clutterbuck snuggled down but he thought longingly of the days when he was a tiny piglet and he wished Sally could wrap him up like a doll and rock him in the old rocking-chair by the kitchen fire. But he knew that as he was much bigger than Sally those days were gone for ever.

Never mind, he thought, this is a treat, and his tail curled tightly like a corkscrew. This straw on top is just like a duvet. I think I'll burrow in every night and have as much on top as underneath and I'll be as warm as a walnut in its shell.

He licked the remains of the cod-liver oil from round his mouth before he went to sleep. He loved it, you see. Pigs do seem to like the most amazing things to eat and drink.

Chapter Eight

Mr Clutterbuck Jones captures a Burglar

Now on this particular day that I shall tell you about Mr Clutterbuck Jones was so tired from sliding on his trotters, and roly-polying inside a snowball, that even though the snow was on the ground he decided to rest in his sty. There was no one in the farmhouse. Mrs Simpkins had taken the children once again to Holly Knoll and Farmer Simpkins had taken Leo to the north fields. Leo is the Simpkins' dog and he got his name because he is such a marvellous ratter and he is as brave as a lion. Curly and Simeon and Benny, the farm workers, were helping to clear snow from the ditches. The farmer didn't want waterlogged fields when the snow started to thaw and the ditches were there to drain the fields.

It is a pity that Farmer Simpkins did not leave Leo in the farm kitchen to guard the farmhouse. I know you have guessed what happened and you are right.

The burglar had come from far away and had already robbed lots of houses in Grassington. When he got to Greendales and saw so many people at Holly Knoll he said to himself: This is my chance to find some empty houses and burgle them. He had taken watches and money from several houses before he reached Willowbrook Farm. The Simpkins only locked the back door at night. During the day, that is until after the burglary, they didn't bother. There was usually someone working near the house and Leo was always around. They knew and trusted everyone in the village. No! They never locked the door until they went to bed.

Mr Clutterbuck Jones, asleep in his bedroom with his red blanket on, snuggled down and snored beneath his straw duvet with his tail curled tightly like a corkscrew. He was having a very exciting dream. Sally had read her geography book to him so often and shown him the pictures that he was simply longing to go to some of those faraway places. He dreamed that he was on a ship sailing across the ocean to the other side of the world. The ship stopped in port and he woke up ready to go ashore with the rest of the passengers. He stepped outside his sleeping-quarters and the dream had been so good that he couldn't believe he was still inside his own pigsty. His tail uncurled sadly. Miss Prudence Daintyways from next door spoke to him through the fence.

'I'm going to stretch my trotters for a while. Coming?'

I might as well, thought Clutterbuck. It will get my blood circulating and you never know, I might find a tasty morsel somewhere. Aloud he said, 'I'll be glad to accompany you, Miss Prudence,' and they met outside the open gates of their pigsties.

They stayed in the farmyard where the snow had been cleared and Clutterbuck suggested that they play hide-and-seek to keep warm. They had such fun because it is really hard for a huge, fat pig to find a hiding place.

Where can I hide this time? he asked himself. I've used up most of the suitable places.

He looked around and saw the water-butt near the back door. It is a large wooden barrel that is used to collect rain-water because Mrs Simpkins knows that it is nice and soft for washing hair in. He couldn't get behind it because it is always too close to the wall, but on this particular day the tarpaulin cover from the pick-up truck was folded beside it. As he wriggled under the tarpaulin his tail curled tightly like a corkscrew.

This is one place Miss Prudence will never find me, he thought. I'd better not go to sleep though or I might snore and give the game away.

So he stayed wide awake and just kept one eye peeking from under the cover. He could hear Prudence trotting hither and thither and looking here and there and he giggled to himself because she was looking in all the wrong places.

BUT WHAT WAS THAT? It didn't sound like pig's trotters clicking along. He kept very still under the tarpaulin and watched. He saw a man tiptoe across the yard to the back door. He was carrying a sack and he had a peaked cap pulled low over his eyes so that it wasn't easy to see his face.

He's a burglar, Mr Clutterbuck Jones said to himself, and I am going to catch him.

But how? He wracked his brains until his head ached. THEN HE HAD AN IDEA. He trotted off to find Prudence and bumped into her as she was coming round the corner of the barn.

'Whatever are you doing, Mr Clutterbuck Jones?' Prudence was very prim and proper and she always used his full name. 'I am supposed to be finding you, not you finding me.'

'There is a burglar in the farmhouse, Prudence –' she flung up a trotter in horror as Clutterbuck continued '– and you must help me to catch him.'

He told her his plan and they went to the farmhouse door, pretended to be asleep, and waited.

Inside the farmhouse the burglar stuffed the things he had stolen into his swag-bag as he went from room to room. When it was full and almost too heavy to carry he opened the door just a tiny bit to see if the coast was clear. When he saw two sleeping pigs near the doorstep he smiled to himself.

'If two sleeping pigs is all I have to worry about then I am in the clear,' he said aloud to no one in particular. 'I'll just squeeze past them and be on my way.'

Clutterbuck and Prudence were ready to

put their plan into action. Clutterbuck's heart was beating like a hammer inside him and Prudence's tummy was churning with excitement. The burglar picked up his swag-bag from the kitchen floor and as he turned to go he saw that both pigs were now in the doorway, completely blocking it.

'Shoo, shoo!' he yelled.

They didn't move. He tried pushing them. He couldn't move either of them by one centimetre, they were so big and heavy.

'I'll have to climb over them,' he muttered.

But as soon as he lifted his foot to step on them Clutterbuck and Prudence stood up quickly on their trotters and tilted the burglar into the kitchen. He picked himself up and rubbed his bruises. Again and again he tried to squeeze past or climb over, but Clutterbuck and Prudence completely blocked the doorway. They snorted and squealed at the burglar. They curled their snouts and showed their small sharp teeth. They stamped their trotters and waved their tails like starting handles on a tractor. They really did look very fearsome, I can tell you.

The burglar didn't want to get too close to the angry pigs so he took a sweeping-brush and tried to push them from the doorway with it. But it was like trying to move two mountains. Clutterbuck and Prudence would not be moved. A song that he had heard Sally sing was going round in Clutterbuck's head:

> *We shall not, we shall not be moved,*
> *We shall not, we shall not be moved.*
> *Just like the tree that's standing by*
>   *the waterside*
> *We shall not be moved.*

The burglar didn't know how he was going to get out. He went to look round the rest of the house. Clutterbuck looked at Prudence. They were both thinking the same thing. What if he found another way out?

The burglar went to the front door but it was locked. He went to every single window in the farmhouse but the farmer had just had them all double-glazed and they were all locked, so there was no way he could get out of those.

I've just got to move those stubborn pigs, he thought, I'll throw a bowl of water on them. That should move them.

When he got downstairs he couldn't even get into the kitchen, never mind get a bowl of water. I know you have guessed what happened and you are right. Those clever pigs had moved inside the kitchen and were now blocking the dining-room doorway. It was impossible for the burglar to get out.

In the north fields Farmer Simpkins said to his men, 'Come on, let's go for a warm-up. Mrs Simpkins left soup simmering for us. How about a big bowlful each?'

When he reached the farmhouse with Simeon, Curly and Benny, the farmer was jolly pleased that it was such a cold day that they had needed warming-up.

With four strong men and two enormous pigs the burglar knew he was caught and he sat down quietly to wait for the police to come. Farmer Simpkins telephoned Police Constable Fred Kettle at the village police house to come and arrest the burglar. Clutterbuck and Prudence waited together in the farmyard.

Constable Kettle was snoozing with his thumbs hooked round his braces when the telephone rang. As he listened to Farmer Simpkins he felt very important indeed. He had been waiting for something like this to happen all his life. You see, he had never arrested anyone before. There aren't any crooks in happy Greendales where everyone knows everyone else.

'Elsie,' he shouted to his wife, 'polish my boots, find my helmet, brush my tunic, get my belt. Quick as you can.'

His wife looked at him calmly and said, 'Haven't you forgotten something?' Just like your mum says to you. He was so excited he didn't know what she meant. But you do, don't you?

'Yes, I've forgotten where my uniform is, so find it quickly.'

'Say please,' said Elsie.

'PLEASE,' roared Constable Kettle, trying to tie his tie with fingers that were all thumbs.

When he was ready and looking as smart as a new pin and not before, he went out of his front door and got on to his large police bicycle. He pedalled as fast as he could. When he came to Holly Knoll he shouted at the top of his voice to everybody as he sped past, 'There's a burglar at Willowbrook Farm. I'm going to arrest him.'

They all left their sledges and ran behind the police bicycle. As they passed the pond, the skaters took off their skates and ran behind the police bicycle. P.C. Kettle felt very important indeed, I can tell you. When he reached the farm he took off his bicycle-clips, smoothed down his uniform, took out his police notebook and police pencil and made himself as tall as he could. He marched into the farmhouse and put one large hand on the shoulder of the burglar and said, 'I arrest you in the name of the law. What have you to say for yourself?' and he licked his police pencil and held it near the notebook, waiting for the burglar to speak. The burglar trembled and shivered.

'I only came in for a warm. I haven't stolen anything,' he moaned.

'We'll see about that,' frowned Constable Kettle. He tipped out the swag-bag and clocks, necklaces and radios scattered on to the table. He was beginning to enjoy himself with all the villagers looking on. 'Take off your coat now, if you please,' he ordered.

And do you know, all the way up the burglar's arms there were wristwatches and bracelets and people began to say, 'That's my watch,' and, 'That's my bracelet.'

The village policeman marched the burglar off to the police house and the villagers patted Clutterbuck and Prudence and made a great fuss of them.

'You saved our precious things. We must reward you. What would you like?'

Mr Clutterbuck Jones knew exactly what he would like. He looked round for Sally for she was the only one who would understand him. He nuzzled his snout in her hand and walked to the television set and back to Sally. He did this several times until Sally shouted, 'I know what he wants. He wants a television in his sty. He's always trying to peep at this one through the window.'

The people of Greendales laughed and laughed. No village had ever had such an intelligent pig before and they were very proud of him.

'Whoever heard of a pig having a television?' said Farmer Simpkins. 'Oh well, he can have the old portable, I suppose. It is a push-button and he can easily push it on and off.'

Clutterbuck's tail curled as tight as a corkscrew and a little song went round in his head:

> *I can't go to school,*
> *They won't have me,*
> *But I can learn a lot*
> *By watching TV.*
> *I'll learn my sums*
> *And my ABC,*
> *And all about countries*
> *Across the sea.*

Chapter Nine

Mr Clutterbuck Jones joins the Carol Party

Now on this particular day that I shall tell you about, sweet treble voices were filling the village school. Mr Johnson the church organist was rehearsing the children's carol programme with them.

He is known as Mr 'Oh-be-Joyful' Johnson because he loves music so much that when he isn't playing the church organ or the school piano he is singing or humming away happily to himself. And on this day so near to Christmas Mr 'Oh-be-Joyful' Johnson was bursting with happiness. You see there is nothing in the world that he likes better than children's voices singing *Away in a Manger*.

His mouth curved into a smile as he played the piano and listened to the lovely carol. Miss Brown the schoolteacher had a lump in her throat, because it always makes her feel like crying even though she hears it sung in her classroom every Christmas time.

In the playground beneath the classroom window Mr Clutterbuck Jones tapped out the rhythm with one trotter.

I wish I could sing, he thought, it is such a happy thing to do.

I know you are wondering what he was doing in the playground. Well, it is quite simple. He was there to hear the children singing. When Dominic, Shar and Sally set off to carol practice Clutterbuck waited until they were out of sight and then he too trotted off to the school. You see he liked carol practice as much as the children did and as he listened his tail curled tightly like a corkscrew and we all know that meant he was happy.

'We want some new ideas this year,' Mr 'Oh-be-Joyful' Johnson was saying to the choir, and Clutterbuck listened intently. 'We want to make even more money than usual to buy many more presents for those who can't afford a jolly Christmas. Will you go home and think about it?'

In all the little village halls and in Grassington Town Hall, the hospital, and the old people's home, everyone loved the Greendales carollers and looked forward to their Christmas concert. The children worked hard and they took happiness wherever they went. The money they collected bought things for old, sick and lonely people.

Under the window in the playground Clutterbuck was thinking hard, THEN HE HAD AN IDEA.

With his tail curled as tightly as a corkscrew he trotted back to Willowbrook Farm as fast as his four little trotters would carry him. He went to his sty and waited. He knew

Sally would come. Ever since she had started school she had taken her readers to Clutterbuck's sty and leaning on his low wall she had practised reading aloud. She didn't stop when she became a good reader and she still takes her problems as well as her happy thoughts to Mr Clutterbuck Jones. Sometimes he can even show her the answers. He waited. Sally came.

'Oh Clutterbuck, I know you can't help me this time, but I'll tell you anyway,' and she told him the choir needed a new idea.

Clutterbuck loved the story of Baby Jesus that Sally had told him so many times. He especially loved the part where all the animals around the manger were as welcome as the three kings and were actually there when Jesus was born.

Yes, he thought, animals are part of the Christmas story, but how can I tell Sally my idea?

In the very old, greystone barn, just down the lane, Farmer Simpkins keeps some of the things his father and his grandfather used to farm the land with long ago. Many farmers leave machinery to rust in the fields in ugly piles. Not Farmer Simpkins. His greystone barn tells stories from the past and he and his men lovingly clean and paint everything every year.

Mr Clutterbuck Jones nudged the back of Sally's legs with his long snout. She knew him so well she knew exactly what he was trying to tell her. He wanted to take her somewhere.

'Lead on, MacDuff,' she said, 'and I'll follow.'

His tail was still curled tightly like a corkscrew as he trotted happily down the lane. He stopped at the barn and nudged the door. Sally opened it and they went inside. He went straight to the yellow and red painted hay-wagon and looked up at Sally.

'Now what are you trying to tell me about the haywain?' Sally asked him.

He tugged her gymslip until she sat down and then he nibbled at her red hair ribbon. She took it off and gave it to him and he carried it in his mouth to the hay-wagon and draped it on a wheel. Then he came back and nibbled the ribbon on the other side and did the same with that. Sally clapped her hands.

'I know!' she said. 'You want us to decorate the haywain for the Christmas carols. What a good idea, Clutterbuck.'

But Clutterbuck hadn't finished. The back of the haywain was down and he walked up into the cart and lay down. This time Sally was really puzzled.

'I'm sorry, Clutterbuck, I simply can't work out what it is you are trying to tell me.'

Clutterbuck's tail uncurled sadly,

How can I make her understand? he asked himself.

He bent his four trotters and knelt on them. He looked up at the roof then down to the ground. Sally couldn't understand. He kept on doing it. Do you know what he was trying to say? Sally knew it was something to do with Christmas carols and all at once she understood. He was pretending to look at the bright star in the sky and then looking at the baby in the manger.

'Of course,' she said, 'you want us to do Baby Jesus in the manger on the haywain. How clever you are, Clutterbuck. Let's run and tell the others.'

Clutterbuck's tail curled tightly like a corkscrew and he thought: Gosh! I do love Sally. She always knows what I mean. And a little song started to go round in his head.

Oh, what a clever pair we are,
I lift my eyes up to the sky
And Sally knows I mean a star.
I turn my eyes down to the hay
And Sally knows just what I mean,
That's where the Baby Jesus lay.

Dominic and Shar were very excited about Clutterbuck's idea and jumped on their bikes to go and tell Mr Johnson all about it.

The haywain was beautifully decorated with green fir branches, mistletoe and holly. Hay was spread all over the floor of the cart. Troddle and Mollups Trestle, the twins who are the village carpenters, built a barn roof and a manger for a baby doll to lie in. Children from the choir were dressed up as Mary, Joseph, the shepherds and the kings. They knelt round the manger and one or two animals nestled in the straw, including Mr Clutterbuck Jones of course. The rest of the choir stood in front of the haywain every time it stopped in market places and on village greens.

Mr 'Oh-be-Joyful' Johnson accompanied the choir very softly on his piano accordion and Troddle and Mollups played a carol on their carpenters' saws in the interval.

Never had Greendales choir been enjoyed so much by so many people. All thanks to Clutterbuck's good idea.

With the happy shouts of 'Merry Christmas' ringing in his ears he snuggled happily under his straw duvet and slept soundly all night.